Quiet please.

Project Boast

29 Poets

eds. Rachel Bentham & Alyson Hallett

tp

Triarchy Press

Published in this first edition in 2018 by:
Triarchy Press
Axminster, England

info@triarchypress.net
www.triarchypress.net

A catalogue record for this book is available from the
British Library.

Printed by TJ International, Padstow, Cornwall

ISBN: 978-1-911193-41-8

Acknowledgements

The editors would like to thank the poets in this anthology for their poems and permissions given to reprint poems that have already been published. They would like to thank Tom Williams for all the amazing work he has done on designing the book. Thanks also to everyone who works consciously and fearlessly towards creating a more equal society for all.

All profits from this book will be given to the Malala Fund.

Contents

Introduction

We began this project because of Sarah Guppy, a Victorian engineer and inventor who lived in Bristol. One of the things she is best known for is devising a bridge without arches or sterlings that was less at risk of being washed away. Her contribution to the design of the suspension bridge in Bristol is widely debated, and as yet seems to be inconclusive. We do know, however, that she had conversations with Brunel and went on to make models for some of his designs.

Sarah Guppy also designed a samovar that made tea and cooked eggs; a method for preventing barnacles from clinging to a ship's hull (this barnacle buster was taken on by the Royal Navy and proved financially rewarding for Guppy); and an exercise bed for women to use at home as it was considered inappropriate for women to exercise in public.

There are no statues of Sarah Guppy, no plaques that recount her inventions. In our culture, it has often been deemed acceptable for women and their achievements to be buried, covered over, dismissed. Sarah Guppy herself once said: *it is unpleasant to speak of oneself – it may seem boastful particularly in a woman.*

Mary Beard's fantastic book, *Women & Power, A Manifesto*, traces the history of women being discouraged from speaking in public spaces all the way back to Homer. Speaking is a gendered issue, and we wanted to ask if this was still the case. Are women still finding that it's unpleasant to speak of themselves? Are we still self-censoring for fear of being judged as boastful? How much has really changed?

It became our dream to put together an anthology of poems by a wide range of women poets responding to these questions. We wanted to create an anthology whose platform is generous and far-reaching, a space where poets could approach the idea of speaking in whatever way appealed to them. Thus *Project Boast* was born. Subjects range from Rome to the dawn chorus, from a mad cow to confessions, from catabolic women to a weasel. Some poets remarked how hard it was to speak of themselves. Some let rip with a formidable self. Some take an inventive approach, while some speak through their poems with a direct, quiet authority.

We wanted to provoke all these voices, to seek them out and encourage them. We wanted to suggest that confidence can come from speaking out. We wanted to update Sarah Guppy's assertion to: *It is good for women to speak of themselves – it is life-changing and vital for a healthy society and culture.* If we can do this, we might see statues and plaques of all the forgotten women starting to appear in our cities. We might begin to address the things that need to be addressed and take another step along the long, long road to equality.

Rachel Bentham & Alyson Hallett

Preface

On Boasting

I know that boasting is wrong. But like so many wrong things, that has never stopped me from doing it. My dad was a boastful man and as a child I thought that the point of every anecdote was to present yourself in a beaming light and, at the end, prove how witty and remarkable you were and how you'd gotten the better of the other fella. In later years, once my son was diagnosed as being on the autistic spectrum, I realised that Dad was too, and that I was probably somewhere close by. Those on the spectrum share a misunderstanding of social clues. Aha! My saving grace. I didn't know or understand that women were supposed to put themselves down. I didn't know that an essential characteristic of being female was modesty.

I remember finding out. I was teaching a Creative Writing workshop. During the introductions one woman said that she was 'probably hopeless and much too old' to be giving writing a go. The group laughed but I was aghast. I mentioned that I thought words mattered and had always tried to use the most exciting, saucy and favourable ones to introduce myself. A man in the group immediately piped up with: "Oh but most men prefer a self-deprecating woman." He then mentioned that he was her husband. (No doubt coming along to make sure she didn't express herself too much). I blushed and managed to hold my tongue for two minutes while I felt chastened, but I have to admit that the shame of being what most men don't prefer didn't last long.

Maybe the days when women have to stand looking in a mirror in a Ladies loo, trying to out-do one another in self-criticism are behind us. ('Oh God look at my hair…' 'Your hair? Just look at my thighs/fat bum/spots.') There was a Maya Angelou poem I loved: 'Phenomenal woman, that's me… '. I met Maya Angelou once (1985, I interviewed her for *Spare Rib*) and of course I found her pride not shameful or something to be judged, but inspirational.

Here are many other phenomenal women speaking of themselves. Speaking up, speaking out. Enjoy…

Jill Dawson

Poetry Permissions and Credits

Many thanks to the publishers and poets for permission to reprint the following poems in this anthology:

'My Mother Pictured Amongst Tobacco Leaves', by Nazand Begikhani, was first published in *Bells of Speech* (Ambit, London, 2006)

'We Prayed for a Man Without a Beard', by Judy Brown, from *Crowd Sensations* (Seren Books, 2016)

'The Confessions', by Judy Brown, from *Loudness* (Seren Books, 2011)

'Turning Fifty', by Anne Caldwell, from *Painting the Spiral Staircase* (Cinnamon Press, 2016)

'Premature', by Anne Caldwell, from *Talking With The Dead* (Cinnamon Press, 2011)

'Hipster Central' and 'Do Nothing', by Lucy English, from The Book of Hours poetry film project: http://thebookofhours.org

'Wildwood' by Deborah Harvey, from *Breadcrumbs* (Indigo Dreams, 2016)

'The Time It Takes To Set'; 'No, I Do Not Tango'; 'Terms And Conditions' by Tania Hershman, from *Terms & Conditions* (Nine Arches Press, 2017)

'RP RIP', by Alwyn Marriage, won the Leeds Peace Poetry Prize in 2015.

'Nancy's Star Turn', by Alwyn Marriage, was shortlisted in the Poetry on the Lake competition, 2016.

'Spared' was written by Katrina Naomi when she was writer-in-residence at the Arnolfini, in response to the exhibition 'Emotional Archaeology' by the artist Daphne Wright. 'Spared' was first published on the Arnolfini website.

'Dawn Chorus', by Janet Paisley, from *Sang fur the Wandert* (Luath, 2015)

'Words for My Daughter'; 'Don't Say You Love Me, Daddy', by Janet Paisley, from *Alien Crop* (Chapman, 1996). This book was shortlisted for the Saltire 1996 Scottish Book of the Year.

'Objets Sacrés de Jeanne d'Arc' and 'The Apostle, Mary Magdalene', by Julie-ann Rowell, from *Voices in the Garden* (Lapwing, 2017)

'Greenham Common, 1985', by Julie-ann Rowell, from *FURIES: an anthology of women warriors* (For Books Sake, 2014)

'The Mad Cow Talks Back', by Jo Shapcott, from *Her Book: Poems 1988 - 1998* (Faber & Faber, 2006)

'Masks', by Penelope Shuttle, from *Unsent* (Bloodaxe Books, 2012)

'I often think', by Penelope Shuttle, from *Will You Walk A Little Faster?* (Bloodaxe Books, 2017)

'The Walk' by Claire Williamson, from *Visiting the Minotaur* (Forthcoming, Seren, 2018)

'Confession', by Arundhathi Subramaniam from *Where I Live: New and Selected Poems* (Bloodaxe Books, 2010)

'Sergei Kuriokhin Wasn't My Lover' by Victoria Field, from *Olga's Dreams* (fal publications, 2004)

What cannot be said
will be wept

Sappho

Caroline Carver

self-puff

when you put brown paper bag on head
breathe in and out
paper go away   come back   go   come back
make cave in place where mouth should be
that is self-puff

when you lie in boat   small boat   on your back
look up at darkness   easy cloud   star maidens
run your hand over side   pull shining alchemy
from water   your mouth small O of pleasure
that is self-puff

when moon lie upside down on sand
shine through glow water
back and forth trembling   of glow water
when you hug yourself because you make sea magic
that is self-puff

when wisps of thought shape themselves on bow
and that wisp is you   only you
that is self-puff *magnifico*

Fiona Hamilton

If Hestia had Designed a Backbone for Atlas

It was a challenging brief.
But not beyond me.
Not at all.

My early sketches were many-antlered beasts,
staircases that rotate and evaporate,
butterflies with teardrop abdomens and long arms.

My first 3D models were
spaghetti-slippery
or ultra-rigid.

I went back to the drawing board
and returned to simple shapes:
the drum, the arch, the star.

I noticed that aggrecan absorbs water
and will distribute hydraulic pressure
in all directions.

In the end I went for thirty-three interlinking
calcium pieces separated and connected
with gel-filled cushions.

Threading multi-track communication systems
down a central flexible column
isn't easy. Cladding has to be state-of-the-art.

I've rolled it out to humans
with some improvements: increased height,
shorter, more integrated buttresses.

I ironed out a few design issues
caused by environmental factors
and changing lifestyles.

Atlas can retire.
This is world class.
It'll hold up, you can be sure.

Hestia, Greek goddess of architecture as well as hearth and home.

Alyson Hallett

Mrs Guppy

Imagine a house late at night,
candle burning, a fever of moths
about a flame. Now see inside

her brain – a woman in a man's
world but only in name. After six
children she can play any game.

The last thing a bridge needs
is to be swept away and so she
designs one minus arches

and sterlings – a suspended road,
flood-proof, torrent-proof, every
bridge-crosser safe. She was born

to invent, to make the unmade.
Who else designed a barnacle buster
for the British navy? Who else

devised a way to cook eggs
in a kettle's steam, an exercise bed
for women forbidden to stretch

in public? Sarah Guppy. She shows
us a world as big or small as we make it,
as bright or dull as we dream.

Anne Caldwell

Turning Fifty

Thus, though we cannot make our sun stand still, yet we will make him run.
~ Andrew Marvell

The field is full of light, air thick
with buttercups, bees, with June heat.
I could lounge in the meadow
until my skin is stamen-yellow,

hair – wet as grass; listen to the chaffinch
on the wire, heart about to burst,
calling for its mate. I wonder what
this mid-life point is all about?

I could Hammerite the spiral staircase
in my yard, I could twitter or tweet,
march for the women of Afghanistan,
or students on the scrap heap,

plant dahlias in terracotta pots
and marvel at their psychedelic blooms
or choose a younger lover, fuck him silly,
then scrub the sheets.

I could buy a Royal Enfield motorbike,
feel it throbbing on the street.
Time's a gyroscope humming on a string;
a cat out hunting when its dish brims with milk.

Nazand Begikhani

Journey With My Jewish Friend

Thanks to poet James Fenton

To Nira Yuval Davis
I invited her to my country
And she said she was not sure to be able to go
As she was born in Tel Aviv

Let's go and visit my country, my friend
But don't tell me of your birthplace
Our lands have caused suffering

And I find it difficult to hide my tears
When I read in my passport
Nationality undetermined
Let's go and make our visit
We are together on this journey

Yes, I am angry by the way I have been defined
And grieve the politics
That shaped my existence
I admit I have been confused,
Longing for a piece of land
I am not allowed to name
Let's go and make our visit, my friend
For we are together on this journey

Do you mind if we don't talk of war?
And keep a distance from their borders
When divided
With our spirits far away from our bodies
What can bring us together?

Yes, I find it hard to connect to a world
That denies my existence
Where do I belong?
Oh, please don't talk to me of war
Let's go and make our visit, my friend
For we are together on this journey

Do you mind if we don't tell the truth
When stopped at checkpoints in Istanbul?
And I promise I will not tell your truth
When questioned at passport control in Iraq
Let's go and make our visit, my friend
For we are together on this journey

Did you say these are clichés?
But you see, we are bound by them.
Where do you come from? They asked.
I can't answer this question, I said.
For I am Kurdish.
You can't answer the question
For you are Jewish.
Let's just go and make our visit, my friend
For we are together on this journey

Jean Hathaway

Pewley Down (1982)

By walking with friends
I've learned the names
To give to plant and tree
To tumulus and field bank,
Cumulus and nimbus,
Greensand, marl, and clunch.

But it's by walking alone
That I've learned to love them.

Dikra Ridha

Home

King Hammurabi's land, I write while you still breathe
to tell a truth, since time and miles have gone to sleep.

Summer jasmines hide in the shade of your palms
and dying leaves fall on you like autumn salaams.

When I call and listen, I don't hear your voice, but a space
speaks of a burning between the hours, pining for embrace;

I saw you with infant eyes and hid you behind the stars –
it was you who saw me arrive and land on your sands.

Law and the poems aside, how do I tell you about the land?
A millennia of seedlings hang on your breath, motherland.

Victoria Field

Sergei Kuriokhin Wasn't My Lover

Last night I dreamt of Russia, rivers,
and how ten years ago those fingers
didn't play my breasts, my sex or my skin,

although I know how they longed to.
Your show thrilled me with its loud and mocking mix
of rock and goats and marching bands – sheer noise aroused me, as did

the naked men who posed as statues round the walls
of pompous St George's Hall.
They winked at me so I took them home and had them all.

I'd die if I didn't see you again – the next night
swopping leather for earnest beards, I watched you play jazz at the Bluecoat
but spent the concert in your Petersburg flat

having you enter me time after time.
Forgetting the keys, you lifted my lid, plucked all of my strings,
your bow roaming over all of my selves,

shouting as you ran up and down
my soft bones
and down and up. It was winter, or summer,

in any case, the window was blank and white.
Anna Akhmatova couldn't sleep for the noise,
threw Modigliani's red roses

across to us lovers and I trailed the petals
when I left, getting lost in the yards within yards,
resting outside the Museum of Atheism,

my sex sore from your symphonic flourishes.
Four fluffy-faced boys see my jeans and approach.
Smoke On the Water? asks one.

Yes I say. Free love? asks another
and I plunge my tongue into his mouth, tasting vodka and bitter tobacco.
Ten years ago,

more or less, more and less,
I tell the woman who asks what I dream.
She's in love with me

and though she'd never say, the sun goes in
when I leave at the end of an hour.
I tell her, Sergei was just the first of thousands

of my Russian lovers, in cities where rivers flow one way
and poetry pulls in the other.
I had them under the bells

of the ancient churches and took them deep in their woods
among insect-loud birches.
Once at the Bolshoi, I bribed the attendant well,

made a nest from the furs then
fucked through Giselle.
Anais Nin, another of my lovers,

only lies when the truth needs improving.
I've never needed to. Today, Radio Three dreams with me –
tonight's Impressions will feature Sergei

(The soft chimes of your fingers on the keys)
Kuriokhin and his legacy to jazz.

Deborah Harvey

Blooded

Then let's blind this tyranny of mirrors
blunt the blades of our bright pink plastic razors

Let's not be neat, compact, discreet
hide who we are in the palms of our hands or up our sleeves

We'll smear our foreheads, noses, cheeks
not with the blood of hunted creatures, stain of killing sprees

but with our blood, this ferrous musk
fecund, nurturing, the russet of red fox

vixen-masked, in long soot gloves
we'll blaze our clamorous ways through scrub

burn ash paths through suburbs, towns
singe the edge of meadows, commons, forests, downs

scratching sparks from burnt-out stars
chasing flames that leap from heart to heart

In Naturalis Historia, *Pliny the Elder says that if a menstruating woman walks
barefoot through fields at sunrise, with her hair dishevelled and her girdle loose,
the crop will wither and dry up. Her glance at this time will dim the brightness of
mirrors and dull the edge of steel.*

Rachel Bentham

the trouble with you is you won't be told

all my life I've
been told. shhh

don't fuss. don't
speak out of turn.

for centuries,
we've been told:

don't stick your neck out
don't raise your voice

don't make a show
of yourself now.

don't you go getting
ideas young lady

don't be too big
for your boots.

now I buy the boots
with my earnings

they fit perfectly.

Judy Brown

The Remove

I always drew close
to the girls whose colours were off
unkiltered from the usual palette
or the boy turning aside
in the school photo. Always
one huge light burning off his glasses,
his angled teeth tamed by wire.

I always drew close
to the man in the greasy monkey jacket
with a touch of green in the cloth, like a fly in the sun.
I could tell he was the one,
leaning forward to greet a stranger.
His ears were red. Drinking
all afternoon had laid him right open.

I always draw close:
there's less responsibility,
nothing but blocked pores,
and the uneasy placating smile.
No need to ask about backstory,
the four sisters all kept home but one,
and her keeping her distance from the other girls
in the long, unheated dormitory.

Penelope Shuttle

Masks

The child has masks.
It is easy to forget this.
Behind her masks
of today and tomorrow
is yesterday's face,
see, she is still too young
to understand anything
but food and sleep.
My threats are no way
to break her silences,
to curb her fires,
there must be a way
of speaking
that runs true and clear
from the womb's infant
to the child who faces the world,
her school masks of fear and pride
sprouting fresh each day;
she flinches but does not retreat;
she wears a bruised lazy-mask,
a stiff oldfashioned anger-mask,
one summer mask glitters, gifted with speech,
another is a poke-tongue laughter mask.
She has her heroic silver bedtime mask.
My own pedantic mother-mask watches.

There must be a language
for me to speak, for her to utter;
a language where the sweet and the bitter
meet; and our masks melt,
our faces peep out unhurt, quaint as babies.

Alwyn Marriage

Nancy's Star Turn

We were five years old, newly-fledged to school,
shy, except for one girl with pretty yellow curls

who spoke loudly and cheerfully in a strange
accent, didn't defer to teachers or avoid the boys,

but when we gathered to drink our third of a pint
of milk at break time, climbed onto a desk

(it wasn't even her desk) and raising her squeaky
voice in a shrill rendering of Nelly the Elephant

proceeded to click and tap the heels
of her impossibly shiny patent leather shoes

in a dance whose fierce percussive beat
thrilled our innocence, suggesting there were worlds

wider and more exciting than our own,
of which Nancy knew but we could only dream.

Rachel Bentham

The Wood and the Trees

May your soul be at home where there are no houses.
~ Ursula K Le Guin

The forest in me knows
the comfort of that quietness
bringing together
the peace and the song there,
the shifting of light,
the company of tall
silent beings.

The forest in me knows
that I belong
in the wood,
that I am alone
in the woods and
replenished
there.

Even when a stranger comes
I am still
and unafraid
because I am the wood.

Nazand Begikhani

A Girl Like Do'a

Will you believe me
If I tell you that I saw a girl
Similar to Do'a
Her body a story
Full of sound and fury

Do'a arising in the city centre
And walking towards me
I am not a saint
Nor Ba'shiqa is a shrine
That was Do'a
Arising in the town centre
Calling on girls and boys
"Come on
Let's talk to these stones
Each is like a word
Carrying many meanings
Let's meditate
Upon the hidden meaning of the stone"

That was her
Do'a
Arising in the city centre
And walking towards me
Carrying a green basket
Full of twinkling stars
She was dressed in a shirt
Woven with love
And a skirt from her childhood
Her face was full of dreams.

She came towards me
Took a stone out of her pocket
And stretched her arm
Read a prayer
She read a prayer
And the stone split in her hand
Turning into a red sea
The town was awash with stones
Awash with sins
Awash with crimes

Believe me that was Do'a
She was riding a white ship
Combing the pink hair of the waves
Flying higher and higher
Circling around
The city centre
And reading prayers
For the safety of the soul of the city.
And the city was full of stones
Stones like the hearts of men
Stones like the eyes of spectators
Stones like the hands of those applauding
Stones like that land of ours
Full of echoes, falling
Full of the smoke of corpses
Full of broken prayers
Like Do'a.

That was her
Doʻa
Coming back from the city centre
She stretched one of her hands

And gave me a stone
A word
That I cannot handle
Nor you can read
Only Doʻa understands the language of stones
She prays for our hands
To speak more softly
Prays for our eyes
To look more kindly
Praying for speech
To create a space of silence.

That was her
A girl like a story
Full of sound and fury.
She was arising in the city centre
Close your eyes and say a prayer
This land is full of Doʻa,
The spirits of Doʻa
She was telling our story
The history of stones.

Kurdistan, October 2013

This poem is dedicated to Doʻa Khalil, a teenage Yezidi girl stoned to death in her village, Baʻshiqa, in Iraqi Kurdistan.

Daisy Proctor

Brush Strokes

Days of Hama beads, loom bands and Beanie Boos' sparkling irises,
squinting through my microscope at veiny fly wings,
spotting Orion's three-starred belt, with my naked eye,
grey antlike cars on the Severn Bridge through my telescope.

Days of Bedminster, Ilminster, Chepstow, to and fro
from Daddy's on the M5. Service stations, rest stops,
eating hot baked goods in the back seat. 'What did you
do at school today?' and 'Who did you play with?'

Mummy's tap-tapping on the keyboard. Bedtime
stories in front of the fire. Daisy Meadows' fairies,
Julia Donaldson's skipping rhymes for my little sister.
RE, SPaG, PSHE and assembly.

Cuddling Jellybean, our rescue weasel,
found in a field, abandoned by the gate.
Sitting next to our dog, Milly,
in the window, watching wildlife rush by.

Brexit, Trump and Mexico. The brush strokes
of Georgia O'Keeffe, Kandinsky, van Gogh, Rousseau.
I'm only a little girl, but my life is bigger
than you'll ever know.

Sally Evans

My Field

A lady bank manager told me once, in a time
of few lady bank managers, when I said to her
I was stuck: It will come from what you can do
and it came:

How being belittled is bad for you,
how I could kick-start a man-clogged engine,
how I have a field at the end, how it was connected
to what I could do.

Life flooded in and out and in again,
my children grew, were shod and flew.
I look back without dissatisfaction,
my hens peck at their grain in the garden.

Janet Paisley

Don't Say You Love Me, Daddy

Don't say you love me, Daddy,
then it's all right.
I am your loving daughter.
At night I hide in the cracked wall
making myself. Becoming so small
you do not see that body under you
does not belong to me.
You teach grown up things
and I don't understand any of it
except mother is crazy and blind.
That's why you are unkind to her.
Sometimes, from my hiding place,
I sing a tiny song.
Thin as thread in a needle
my voice is not strong enough
to stitch me well.
I'm a monster who can't tell.
Words would make you real
then I'd feel and I don't, I don't.
Can't move, make a sound now
but when you're not around
I burst your eyes on my nails,
prise your tongue out of my mouth,
shred your skin, stick
the kitchen knife into your heart.
I make hate then, to live on,
and you can't take that too
when I hide it inside a deep wall.
So just don't say you love me,
Daddy. That's all.

Caroline Carver

Hurricane Mama

Saba   I going crash through window with eyes wide open
speak with mouth full   of   fire   water   soot
smear pig dirt on those nice clean walls you just painted
take my clothes off   my grubby grubby clothes
roll in mud puddles the rain do bring
speak like cow girl   like possessor of bodies
speak with dun language foul language
chicken language heads cut off language   Saba   if they cut my head off
I still keep running

why you try calm me down?

why you speak nice when I rage like Hurricane Mama?

why you no angry?

I hit my head on floor   you still speak to me
I cut my arm   you still speak to me
I cut tablecloth   curtain   counterpane
you still speak to me

no one can fill hole in my head
cure sun-ripped hands

no one can bring my father back to me

but I have memories   you say

is true I have memories

       will   always

the times he threw me in the air
that is a memory
when he smoked his pipe in the evening
that is a memory
when we walked on the beach and he said
say damn   daughter mine *say damn*
that is a memory
when he laughed so hard todies and finches flew out of him
that is a memory

I will not cry any more
I will be quiet as moon shining on water
moon making long welcome road over water
I will tell my mind   go after moon on water

bring me water   Saba
after I walk the moon road   I will sleep

Julie-ann Rowell

Greenham Common, 1985

Everything is monochrome, but for the fire
which she feeds and coaxes like a child,
they can't help but see it, the men behind the wire

who keep guard all year, as if she were a thing gone wild,
which she supposes she is to certain minds
who don't take trouble with, but interrogate this mild

and gentle figure. She is only fending off the cold, inclined
to nothing stronger than a rebel song, a mug of tea,
yet her daughter has forsaken her, to which she is resigned –

principle was never a wedding guest with suitable repartee.
Now anything so formal has no meaning,
there is only this camp, the stolen heath, the wind in the trees,

and the men behind the wire watching
this woman beside a fire dreaming.

RP RIP
Rosa Parks

Contrary to the popular stories, you were not
particularly exhausted from a long day's work,
or even from carrying too much shopping;
but just tired of injustice and of giving in.

A determination you'd never felt before
covered your body like a quilt on a winter's night.
It was a black and white case of breaking the rules,
followed by unexpected consequences.

Like David with his little stone
you found to your surprise
that though you felt so insignificant,
you weren't alone, for thousands more arose

to join the boycott that would stop
the buses, not for one night, or a week,
but for three hundred and eighty one days,
bringing a giant corporation staggering to its knees.

Mother of freedom, who would have thought
you'd lie in state on Capitol Hill?
Against the odds, your disobedience
shifted the axis of the world,

reminding us that sitting still
was once the cause of a great movement,
and breaking rules can sometimes change
the course of history.

Lucy English

DO NOTHING

I will lie in bed and do nothing.
I was dreaming of lino floors and pastel blue cupboards.
A Formica table top speckled like sand.
Lakes and rivers in the lino. Rivers of mud.
My chair was a ship
with a red plastic seat.

If I turn I can open the curtains
with my toe.
I used to think clouds were like pillows.
And the turn of an Easy Jet landing at Lulsgate.
There's a crack in the ceiling looks like a river.
The delta end is near the window.
I'm in a plane looking down at the estuary.

Merging in strands. My hair on the pillow.
I used to think clouds were like pillows.
I jump from the plane and I'm hurtling down.
I'm shocked. Clouds are just water. Droplets of mist.
I fall from the plane and onto my bed.
Soft. I am soft.

Under the covers.
I'm thinking of you. I'm not fifty four.
I'm seventeen and my tummy's flat.
But it's not you. It's my first love.
I stroked his hand and he pulled my panties down.
We did it on the floor. In the car. Behind the shed.
In the garden. On the floor.
But seventeen means too much crying.

He was crying and I was crying.
So I'm not seventeen. I am seven.
The pillow is a snow slope I can jump on.
Tiny me in a snow field.
On a cloud. The sun's gone in.
I was dreaming of a kitchen. Was I?

A red plastic seat?
I'm fifty four and it's my day off.
Get up. Breakfast. Coffee. Toast.

Anne Caldwell

Premature

I'm kept in a box. I blink.
Smell hot plastic. Stretch out my hand
to watch a pattern of light redden.
I'm a glow-in-the-dark; half-fish
with slithery lungs in a ribcage supple as a slipper.
My skull's pointed, yet to harden.
My hold on life is lax.

Mother's face rises like a full moon
and her eyes cloud over with green.
I've lost her metronome heartbeat.
I've no idea of the comfort of her milk-tipped
nipple, nor the crook of her arm,
nor the rhythm of a walk in the park
with sycamore leaves to soften the sun's stare.

Self-Portrait as Katharine of Aragon

I have a queen's reason
    for working my stitch-fingers to the bone
        as summer dims in green corners of England

and the radio's bedside manner blesses the air
    Wild rose, wild rose, was once my call sign
        I always loved the Spanish-speaking world

but heads and tails of silence drift into the chamber
    where I embroider time-lord clouds
        hiding sun and moon

remembering from the future that when a military plane
    finds itself in serious trouble
        the voice command switches to the feminine

But why let the future be more than my servant,
    sent to do my bidding centuries from now?
        Don't tell me the future sits on the floor,

the place for beggars or for one out of her wits
    The future is simply a way of hiding my heart within my own heart
        bruised and bound as it is, ruling neither Commons nor King

They say the peony or Benedictine Rose was sold
    for one hundred ounces of gold,
        they say nettles also sit in the rose genus

        They say the axe has been ordered from France

Cara Squires

i am a work of art

i am a work of art
i am a work of art
and you can't break my heart
anymore
and i think i used to care about you
but i don't do that
anymore

i am a constellation
exploding across the sky
i am a neon sign that reads
passion, devotion, excellence
my words could launch ships
change lives
i can do anything i set my mind to

you are describable in one word
mundane
you have no idea who you are
you don't strive
you were not worth the effort
but i made it anyway

because i was kind and optimistic
i believed in love and hope
still do
nobody as bland as you
could take that away from me

i know myself
i am brave and caring
i am honest and loud
i believe in people and comedy
crying and laughing and being alive
i know who i am
i know who i am and i'm not yours

i don't want to be
i certainly don't need to be
because i am a work of art
and you can't break my heart
anymore
and i think i used to care about you
but i don't do that
anymore

Clare Shaw

My Father Was No Ordinary Man

My father could fly. He needed no father –
he had mother, the hunger of four older brothers –
my father was one of an army of brothers
and he learnt all the ways of men.

My father was handsome and worshipped by women.
His loins were a river: they flowed with his children
and he was the fountain of truth we all drank from
and when he held forth we would not interrupt him.
My father named every flower in the garden,
each star in the night by the right constellation.
He knew all the birds by their song

and they sang it. My father could never be wrong.
His hands were a gun and they brought down the rabbit.
He fed us on flesh that was studded with bullets.
There was fire in his fist, there was gold in his pocket.
My father turned water to wine and he drank it –
he needed no prayer and no God

for he was the word and he rang like a hammer.
Oh, my father was victor; he rode on our shoulders,
he rode deep inside us. We carried my father
through hell and high water,
we proved ourselves worthy of love

and his love was a river in flood.
The sun made him happy.
The truth was soft mud in his hands, oh truly
he was the truth and he was the glory.

He filled all the rooms with his song and his story,
his whisper could silence a house

for my father bore pain that you could not imagine.
His forearms were scarred and his fingers were broken.
His lungs were a pit and his heart was a puncture.
Oh, my father was hard and my father was tender
and his hand was a mark
we will all wear forever.

Janet Paisley

Dawn Chorus

In the early morning plants are silver,
catching grey light before there is light
while earth lingers in night-shadow.

A small bird, dark as the ground it hops on
heads for the remains of badger food,
a first silent sign of the world waking.

I wonder whose ghostly garden this is
and why I have not slept this night
or where the dawn is that comes so slow.

It has taken a lifetime to reach this minute,
to a garden that will soon glow, coloured
and flushed with the burst of bloom;

to a birdlife that will chatter the yard
fighting over feeders that are overfull
with enough for all. A curt woodpecker

stained red; bullyboy greenfinches shoving
gold, at sparrows, siskins while great and good,
the aerodynamic tits swoop in. It's been

so long. The sky is rising yellow under
the belly of storm cloud. The senior black cat
at the window wants in. His bookend number

two, likewise positioned, backs to each other.
Facing the frame, they watch me staring out
as the storm glowers waxy candlelike.

In the night, foxes fought with clacking teeth
among carefully cared-for flowers and trees.
Last night I wrestled the tricks and turns

of a life that makes, and feeds, and frets
and does not know when to end-stop
the multiplication of thought and word.

As the garden colours up, the nightshift
slips into envelopes, day unfolds. Now
nothing more can be done but sleep.

Dikra Ridha

Unforgiven

It's a girl. I am sure.
The walk back under charcoal
sky, dragging a sack of kind words; my footsteps
splatter in streaming pavements; no sun
can brighten such days.

She comes to me in the rain
tries to stop a train of sacrifices,
to pull the scale down to her side,
she tells me she chose me.

But the recurring dream had already been signed:
'one lion cub is enough' says a man.
Mud pours into my aura,
rain in my mouth.
The lion cub feels for his sibling –
she tells me: 'choose me'.

There are mums weeping at hospital
doors – only two of us hear their questions.
The lion cub prods my abdomen, he cannot
express a brightness in his eyes, seeing
perhaps, a miniature light.

But the financier in a suit is unhappy:
'one room is enough for two,' he says.
We tell no one.
Plant a tree.
Say sorry.

'Chiara' she tells me.
'Chiara' in her apricot T-shirt. Only I
hear her questions. A three-petalled daisy
lies in her chest.

In the morning,
the lion cub splashes in puddles;
I remove my earrings
and go to sleep. When I wake
he comes to me and weeps.

Katrina Naomi

Spared

I have found seven hearts
        lost one   found six more   They hang
like Xmas decs on a wedding tree so much bad
        wallpaper   And I'm unsure
if I'm indoors   or out
        The trellis shifts
for some unseen bird that comes
        like a suitor
not one you'll welcome
        if you know what I know
A normal asylum then this
        a century of roses and killer-birds
all too ready to tip breathing hearts
        from the nest   for these are the rules
of marriage   Such a common
        selective   madness
wisdom   caught on a white rose briar   So brittle
        this pale domesticity   I could snap
your wishbone   White crowds
        a room   walls unable to march
back or forth   And so many choose
        this space   where all ties are
severed for the ice and snow
        of love   its crazed pattern
of fracture and fall
        Every girl's dream   for a veil
to render her beautiful   as we fail
        to look a suitor in the face
for we have been sold   Nothing
        here is straight   We see shadows
of ourselves   the door slowly barred

with so much love   There is no such thing
as claustrophobia   Trust me
        I am perfectly safe here   can only hear
one bird   the killer-bird   out of season
        its suitor voice plays
to all the seasons of my life
        an extreme bird then   a favourite
yet you will not find her
        among the neon lights of sky
for I am one to have been
        spared

Alyson Hallett

Miss Ballantine's Salmon

still holds the record for being the largest
Atlantic salmon caught in British waters. Yes,

in 1922 Miss Georgia Ballantine reeled in
the king of the cold seas and brought him

to shore. Mr Malloch cast the fish
to preserve the tale then Miss B dispatched it

to Perth Royal Infirmary for staff and patients
to eat. What a feast. What a fish. What a woman.

Sally Evans

Staying Power

I take it you don't want
a c.v.? I'll never grovel
for some position where overlords
could sack me any time.

I take it you want an account
of adventures, places I have not just seen
but revolutionised. Countries I have overcome,
potentates I have subdued.

Whole libraries I have read,
subjects I have swallowed,
actual and honorary academic degrees.
Ask me some other time.

More likely you enquire
how I've raised children, pacified my men,
sent them all shining clean
into society.

Think again. I'm most proud
of what I stuck through that went wrong,
the smile that stayed on my face,
words I wrote and still write,

when people come to me
bring me their half-hidden sorrows,
thank me for having understood,
hug me but do not kiss –

My staying power my success.

Jennifer Wong

Crossing

What if I don't sign a landing card? How about
if I make my way to the main queue?
And every time, the questions

why are you here   and for how long.
The officer peers at my place of origin
through the looking glass, his eyes cold and clinical.

Does he know what I've left behind: Cantopop,
a ricecooker, and a job too good to miss
(Jimmy Choos and a chauffeured Toyota)?

I have disobeyed Confucius:
I've left my parents behind
who grow old in another country.

I've read Chaucer and Ancrene Wisse;
can make fish pies (the Mary Berry way).
If I have a garden, I might do some gardening.

Silent and grim, he flips through
each page of my passport, before leaning forward:
how do you say you look pretty in Mandarin?

Lineage

I was nine months pregnant, and waiting, when the man in the
Taranaki airport shop snapped *this isn't a library you know,*

and when I turned my great belly full of fingernails and teeth-in-bud
towards him he asked (hotly) if I was *actually* going to *buy* anything.

The baby made exclamation marks with its soft bones,
glared with its wide open eyes – two Os. *No* I said *I won't buy*

my news from you. Above the town, Mount Taranaki blazed red and then
in the quick cold dusk the plane with my parents in, touched down.

That night the child swung from its treehouse to the tree
and climbed through me to my mother's hands and with its

persimmon tongue brought us stories (both good and terrible)
from this world, and the other one.

Arundhathi Subramaniam

Confession

To take a homeopathic approach to the soul is to deal with the darkness in ways that are in tune with the dark. ~ Thomas Moore

It's taken time
to realise
no one survives.
Not even the ordinary.

Time to own up then
to blue throat
and gall bladder extraordinaire,

to rages pristine,
to guilt unsmeared
by mediocrity,

to separation traumas
subcontinental
and griefs that dare
to be primordial.

Time to iron out
a face corrugated
by perennial hope,

time to shrug off
the harlotry
and admit
there's nothing hygienic
about this darkness –
no potted palms,

no elevator music.
I erupt from pillars,
half-lion half-woman.

The floor space index I demand
is nothing short
of epic.

I still wait sometimes
for a flicker of revelation
but for the most part
I'm unbribable.

When I open the coffee percolator
the roof flies off.

Julie-ann Rowell

Objets Sacrés de Jeanne d'Arc

Five swords
four plain, one of great artistry
recovered from *Sainte-Catherine-de-Fierbois*
on your instructions. You once smote a whore
on the back with it and the king was displeased:
'The sword is anointed as you are.'

A white harness
each piece perfectly moulded to your body,
the greaves, knee plates, hauberk and cuirass,
spaulders and the gauntlets,
the polished breastplate fitted with an *arret de cuirasse*.
A gambeson of horsehair.

The spurs you never required.

Two silver rings.
One from your mother inscribed *Jesu Maria*.
Both confiscated by the English
and most likely melted down.

A white embroidered banner of boucassin
fringed with silk,
worked by careful women in Tours
who kissed every stitch.

Unpicked.

A wooden spoon and bowl you scraped
food from, frugally, burned on the pyre
with your shoes.

The bascinet you wore into battle,
behind glass in a museum in New York City.

Dented.

The plain cross in your tent
though you needed no reminding of God
who lived in the light of the fire
that so happily consumed you.

Lucy English

HIPSTER CENTRAL

Whatever happened to the greasy spoon?
This cafe now does skinny lattes and eggs Benedict for brunch.

Sophie and Matt love it here. Sophie and Matt both thirty four
left London and careers in a hedge fund
to buy Original Edwardian features and a sense of place.
He's now a sustainable development consultant.
She makes jewellery out of vintage glass
which she sells on Etsy. She's branching into wood.

Their home was sound but needed 'colour'.
They sourced stuff from Freecycle
and reclaimed the floor. The antiques add a quirky touch.
They love it here. Especially now baby Io's arrived.
They can get organic cavolo nero in 'Open Ground'.
Another shop sells Spanish Cheese.

I have to say I love it too.
With my skinny latte and my new hipster shoes
I am reading, in German, Rilke's 'Book of Hours'.

Boasting Sonnet

I'm not one to brag but Sharon Olds wrote
me a poem; me from a council estate.

I've done handstands, on a skateboard, downhill
yet failed both Maths and English O level.

I'm still in love with the man I met at
eighteen. I don't believe in marriage but

I once won an award for headbanging
and chaired human rights talks at the UN.

Expelled from school, I'm now a PhD.
I don't wear make up, this is the real me

unless I'm doing panto. In Cornish.
I'm a qualified mountain leader. Wish

you could see my scything and lindyhop.
I'd say much more but sonnets make you stop.

Penelope Shuttle

I often think

or feel
I'm still inside
the heart
There I am
I come and go in there
I look as if I'm outside
the heart
and everything's upfront
and ordinary –
But no
I'm
inside the heart
making the most of it
in spite of everything
coming and going
with my Kindle
my password
and my shopping

There's no time to think twice
only time to know
I'm inside the heart
where it's Thursday
at least one day a week
and I'm getting closer
and closer
to you
despite what people tell me
is the otherwise
but they don't know a thing
about this heart

of ours
do they
and what it can do
without even trying

Rachel Bentham

Dr Bentham is Out of the Office:

she's wading through
damp cemetery grass
with seeds between her toes

she's hoping to see
bees cutting doors from
her rambling rose

she's stroking the down
like a grandmother's cheek
on her unripe peaches

she's in Tahiti
stumbling in French
strolling black beaches

she's up on the roof
stretching and corpsing
saluting the sun

she's dancing a dervish
leaping and wriggling
pure wordless fun

she's gone to Bhutan
to the high mountains
to sit above clouds

she's writing a poem
digging it out
away from the crowds

Tania Hershman

Terms and Conditions

I can't call it mine, though I paint its nails my chosen shades, I clean
and feed it. Mostly, it seems satisfied; sometimes I'm woken in the night, stomach complaining. It sits me on this sofa,
walks me to work. Is the agreement hire-purchase? Or am I a hotel guest: sure, make a mess, we'll straighten the sheets
– but don't

      stealfromtheminibar smashamirror riptheTVfromthewall
                 We have your credit card.

When I vacate, who next gets that tiny kettle, the unused shampoos? Will I regret leaving the miniatures untouched?
And will my final sigh be for the fear that wouldn't let me ignore prudence and warning letters, turn the volume up
                  and roar.

Fiona Hamilton

What My Grandmother Tells Me in Dreams

Disturb neat lawns
with boisterous fandangos.

Who says
you get what you deserve?

Don't prostrate yourself
before parking meters.

Beware of those who speak
on behalf of The People.

Replace hurtling and rushing
with suspended slow-motion.

Overthrow obsessions
with how things look. See differently.

Notice the invisible
starting with insects and ice.

Put a spoke in fact-fakery.
Invent a different spinning wheel.

Sit for a while with others
and make something warm

made of real wool. Not fluff.
Master the art of listening.

Passions are as unpredictable
as trade winds. Stand your ground.

Economists are not fortune tellers.
Disturb the soup.

Season your days.
Spice everything with cayenne fire.

Gill Hague

The Tears Come Easy to Kate

The tears come easy to Kate

The churning stomach
The feeling of having no right in this world

You're too fragile, they tell her

Too easily knocked off course
You need to get some backbone, Kate

The tears leap up

When she should be strong
Yes. She knows they're right

She should get that backbone

See, she's wrong again
She knows she is hopeless fragile no good…

--

Yes. Well… No

I am fragile
And that doesn't have to be bad

Thinks Kate at her best

I was fragile when I was little
That was the result of it

Fragile is also human
And to be treasured
Think of a feather or fine silk

She wants to say out loud

Fighting tears. But she can't
Her confidence fails. She's just a coward

--

Yes. Well… No

Sometimes she feels delicate and proud
Then they tell her she should have nurtured

A safe place inside her

When she was young
Like other people. Yes

But she didn't. It just wasn't possible

Her fault, another failure
No backbone and no safe place either

--

Yes. Well… No

She feels inside she's tried her very best
She knows fragile is also human

And to be treasured

She feels delicate and proudly beautiful
Precious. And she is

Claire Williamson

Bathurst Pool

July-hot at the lido.
You screech, as at each metal step,
the cold water laps higher up your chest.
I watch. *Can you touch the bottom?*

Cheeks puffed out
you let go of all
that holds you,
except my eyes.

As you sink,
the water breaks
with the tips
of two long strawberry plaits.

Thin arms trail like rushes
failing to crown the surface.
Apple face blurs –
no nose, no mouth.

I peer down, seconds stretching
into our drowned future.
How long will she be?
Come on.

Too late to call the lifeguard,
I jump in beside you
and take hold
of your small body.

My dress billows
on the surface,
then clings, as your in-breath
pulls us gaze to gaze.

she

she can dominate a conversation, steer it in her favour
(she has felt like she may never speak again)
she can smile and laugh and joke
(she has cried oceans, spent nights wide awake)
she can be the last to leave, the life of the party
(she has failed to make it past the front door)
she takes great pleasure in sleeping alone in the centre of her bed
(she dreams of lying curled against another, never feeling alone again)
she feels happiest at a safe authoritative distance
(she wants to be profoundly understood, allowed to be vulnerable)
she is sharp
(she is kind)
she believes in learning from mistakes
(she believes in second chances)
she is too much
(she is not enough)
how can she be each of these things
her very existence is a contradiction
so confused
so layered
so achingly, beautifully human

Deborah Harvey

Wildwood

It's time to leave this house

Glancing up as I cut the grass
I see three apples, green in leaves,
the first-ever crop on the tree I grew
from the seed of the final fruit
picked in my grandmother's garden

I'll watch them swell and ripen
take the pips with me when I go,
plant a tree that might not blossom
in the years that are left

There are millions of seeds in pots and jam jars,
spilling from mouths of paper bags
one for each minute of each day lost,
copses, forests, wildwood
falling through my fingers

I reach for the hands of my children, my sisters,
our dormant stories stir in earth
make for the light

Judy Brown

We Prayed for a Man Without a Beard

'My Tooth broke today. They will soon be gone.
Let that pass I shall be beloved—I want no more'
  ~ **Dorothy Wordsworth**, *Grasmere Journal*, **Monday 31st June 1802**

As the hygienist scrimshaws round my gum
I stretch my small mouth wide as horror.
She learned on a metal skull with white teeth
painted with a black stain to be scraped clean.

When she grew exact, they covered the head
with a rubber sheath – lipped, eared, with hair –
which hugged the mouth's airy cathedral,
its cloisters filled with the breath of winter.

For months a hand scaler was all she held.
In the exams they were tested on people:
We prayed for a person with a big mouth
and small teeth; we prayed for a man without a beard.

I feel my face grow tight, and sickening
as a mask on my skull's frame. After death
rot will strip it down to show the teeth I held,
coddled by the hygienist's intricate decades.

Then the cool breezes off the fells will blow
over the roots. My phantom head smiles:
free at last of the pornography of skin.
I pray for a man to kiss me, while I live.

Rome

We've sung the hymns named
for rain and for punishment,
also the hymn named wrongly,
when it was asked of us.
We've given our eyes
and our breasts,
obeyed The Atlantic and The Pacific,
sworn our names away.
We've listened to silver-tongue words
such as capture and oath,
held our peace about the rewards
and obligations of the flame,
ignus inextinctus.
We have the place of honour.
We hold pardon in our eyes.
We see what the night is
and where the day belongs to the tribe.
We've broken our fall with Caesar's wounds.
We've sung the hymn to ruin.
We've kissed Rome to death.

Alyson Hallett

Here's The Thing

Here's the thing –
> I know my own mind
> I know my own body

Here's the thing –
> Nina Simone didn't want
> to be a singer she wanted
> to be a classical pianist

Here's the thing –
> the paintings of Hilma af Klint
> were rejected by Sweden's
> contemporary art gallery
> for being too spiritual

Here's the thing –
> thousands of unmarried mothers
> were committed to psychiatric
> hospitals for not wearing a ring

Here's the thing –
> the New Zealand poet Janet Frame
> was saved from a lobotomy by winning
> a prize for her short stories (but only
> after more than a hundred shots of ECT)

Here's the thing –
> I know my own mind
> I know my own body

Here's the thing –
> things are changing.

Tania Hershman

The Time It Takes To Set

Not just that you didn't know
who I was

      after all our time together, but that you didn't
      try, weren't curious. I wanted you

to start sentences with *Because I know*
you love x or *y*, but it never happened

      so I left. Finding I didn't know
      myself, I melted

down the bronze, re-cast. I am still
liquid in parts, but oh, the light, the light.

Janet Paisley

Words For My Daughter

Come, the cap of birth is dry,
my labouring is done, your cry
has split the world's roof.

Be comforted, the womb
returns to wrap around you.

Sweet darkness, velvet-blood
from which you came, as night
will cup you again, again

move you outward into light;
a brilliance to be danced in

is life. Your staggering steps
will grow to trust this earth;
it meets both sure and unsure feet.

That shifting pain will shape
the edges that define you.

Know the body that confines
is a new kind of freedom
to find the fullness of you.

Move through yourself. See,
the future is with child

and needs your labouring.
Be done with pasts, walk away.
I'll watch. I'll guard your back,

blinded by my own time. Go forward
from the shadows mothers cast.

As old women shrink, rich fruit
seeds into the garden.
I have been. Now you. So live,

we have both shed our tears
for miracles, for coming new.

In birth-sleep heavy at my breast,
love child, first comes the dream
and then the making true.

Lynn Davidson

Speaking to the Otter

It doesn't break the water to emerge, rather
lifts water into otter-shape.

When it makes itself from river in front of me
I say hello

– the word formless in air, but oh the need to speak
because I am human, immersed in time, and this creature is fleet.

Daisy Proctor

The Wildlife We Found

We rescued a weasel once.
I named him Jellybean.
He couldn't walk, or see
and he had no mummy,

but he became a member
of our family, growing up
so quickly. He learned
to jump from shoulder

to shoulder – over a metre.
He climbed the curtains
and would poke his head
over the rail to squeak 'hello'.
He played hide and seek

with the dog. Sometimes
he went out through
the cat flap. But he always
came back. Until one day,

he made his own way into the world.
Sometimes I look at the cat flap
and know he was the wild
life we found.

Nazand Begikhani

My Mother Pictured Amongst Tobacco Leaves

Your picture in the greenness of the tobacco leaves
reflecting the light of the Orient
you bend among the endless lines
of the staring tobacco plants
like doubt after conviction
you pick up the leaves
lay them in the Charoga
hanging at your neck
and carry them to the Ber Heywan

Piles of sad leaves
Piles of silence
hidden under the Nur of the Orient

Your wrinkled hands
talk to me
tell the story of a stolen childhood
the loneliness of women in my homeland

I look at your fingers
you place the leaves one by one on the tobacco shish
threading them like long beads into a necklace
then you kneel before this heap of tobacco necklaces
place them on your back,
climb the hill to reach the Chardagh
and hang them in precise lines
to dry

Infinite lines of tobacco necklaces
Infinite scars on your heart

I can feel your body drying up
like the tobacco plant in the midsummer heat
and your life
your life similar to the tobacco leaves
has been picked and burnt away
like a cigarette
between a man's fingers.

Fiona Hamilton

Jazz

to be a soul's thrum on a jazz beach
a gleam side of a brass screech
a brash blast in the hot heat

or to glide, slide, and ride the waves
give a slow moan in a dark place

then snap back and syncopate
cascade notes so the air shakes

while the band plays you'll go
counterpoint, holding

low notes, then
lift your voice

to a high note, next
pause
         and sigh

you can lose yourself
(but you don't die)

let your worries go
and the music fly

Jo Shapcott

The Mad Cow Talks Back

I'm not mad. It just seems that way
because I stagger and get a bit irritable.
There are wonderful holes in my brain
through which ideas from outside can travel
at top speed and through which voices,
sometimes whole people, speak to me
about the universe. Most brains are too
compressed. You need this spongy
generosity to let the others in.

I love the staggers. Suddenly the surface
of the world is ice and I'm a magnificent
skater turning and spinning across whole hard
Pacifics and Atlantics. It's risky when
you're good, so of course the legs go before,
behind, and to the side of the body from time
to time, and then there's the general embarrassing
collapse, but when that happens it's glorious
because it's always when you're travelling
most furiously in your mind. My brain's like
the hive: constant little murmurs from its cells
saying this is the way, this is the way to go.

Khairani Barokka

ode to cellulite

marbled joys twist and breathe
outside museums, mausoleums.
full and live. dem thighs.
got behinds like zebras
in shades of brown-beige.

i refuse to let creams capitalise
on the hatred of strangers
for a body that gilds my battles
without complaint, grits its teeth
      into the texture of a grenade.

its teeth in a row look fullness
plumped out, onto skin it goes ridges
flat first, protecting bends,
shielding folds, maximise.
gawk at all these panthera tigris,
      of family felidae.

i striped my own plump
this fine, made it mine.
clamped rainforest
unto a muscle,
strapped tight,
song signs
only natives would know.

fed nourishing sky
from the neck down,
thick clouds form,
subcutaneous heavens.

fed the keys to the kingdom
of plenty,

hips, shin, keratin.

fed large so i could sing.

Julie-ann Rowell

The Apostle, Mary Magdalene

He likes my cool mind. He grows tired
of raised hands and testimonies, weeping
and wailing. Anyone could. You have
to experience it every day to understand
the demands that people make. They want
instant answers. The words he's given
me stretch a long way. Some people
won't pay heed and shout *whore*. It doesn't
matter. It's mostly men with hearts of stone
who don't know what's coming to them.

He likes my cool mind and sometimes
he lays his head in my lap and I stroke
his hair. It's dense between my fingers.
He'll send the others away and they'll go
though they won't like it. I have him all
to myself and I drink his words.
You must carry on, he says, whatever happens.
I want to. I also know I won't be included
if he's not around. They'll wipe me out
or write me down. Change my history.

He likes my cool mind and the way I speak
like a whisper in the wind, he says
but I'm made of iron. I can walk thirty
miles a day and my feet won't weep.
I can out-walk the other disciples.
Children run beside me and grasp my hand.
Women are gladdened. They see me
and think perhaps we do bring peace.

They say: *She wouldn't follow a butcher.*
Watch how she holds your gaze.

Gill Hague

A True Story

She was a child in the First World War.
Lost her brother at 8, her father at 13.
Had to leave school then, to do the skivvying.

Married one of her mother's boarders.
Did what was called for.
Cooked perfect meals daily for the next 60 years.

Nursed the elderly, played cards fiercely.
Always insisted on putting her husband's job first.
He didn't get very far, never promoted.

Full of himself though, she chose to get on with things.
Thought it her duty to help anyone she could.
Was severe if you tried to make her promote herself.

Put you in your place in no uncertain way.
Found it childish, unseemly, if there was any fuss.
She'd have liked that woman bridge engineer.

Always kept the house cold, her hands numb,
Because her husband liked it that way.
Had to go to hospital with hypothermia once.

When she got frail, she went into a nursing home.
Met a lady from the room next door she thought.
"I'm delighted," she smiled. "She's like me, you know."

"We even wear the same clothes."
She was out of character in her enthusiasm.
Saw the lady in the mirror every day.

"She has good judgement like me," she said with pride.
Her life became a pleasure. "We use just the same words,"
"The lady likes it warm like I do."

"We're both strong," she told anyone who'd listen.
"We even look just like each other."
She and the lady lived happily till the end.

Jean Hathaway

Hats (1985)

The phone rings
and as the sound builds up
I hear a rinky-tinky Circus orchestra.
I tightrope walk
the edges of carpets
and the bannisters.

The ground is familiar
so I do not stretch wide my arms
but, for the further amusement
of the non-existent Big Top crowds
I juggle my many hats,
dusting each a little as it passes
through my hands:
a practical one for the Nature Reserve,
something vast and Sackville-West for the writers' group,
a coloured cotton hat, for driving children to the Nursery,
a cosy one for Cruisewatch on winter nights.

Excitement grows,
I find bigger and better hats,
and fling them in the air,
and keep them circling
as I prepare to snatch the very one
and put it on, just the second I find out
who is calling me, and what they're asking for.

The Ringmaster cracks his whip.
It is my husband that they want,
and all my whirling hats fall useless
to the ground:
I kick them away.

Tania Hershman

No, I Do Not Tango

Don't call for me there, I have stepped
off that dance floor, and I am

relieved. Every part of me
is mine, no hand on my shoulder, arm

around my waist, no waiting
for an invitation. A hundred years ago

they would have called me – with those
two million others – surplus, extra. Elizabeth

the First caused similar confusion. No mate,
no children. Virgin Queen, they also named her

Mother of the Nation. Also: Prince. You
can call me anything you like. I know my name.

Judy Brown

The Confessions

At first I was a rattle strung with gold bells.
No one could shut me up, my pink mouth
gabbing pure lies and pulling on a Silk Cut.

Later was quieter. A coral grows round that self,
toughs over the cuckoo-froth and soft stuff.
Some of it wasn't pretty but I tell you: I spat out

nothing, as a gourmande feasts on what she loves.
Now I unwrap it all, lay it on fruitwood tables.
Under halogens, I count the increments of this lust,

despising no denomination: not the smears
from other hands nor the half-split Scottish notes
smelling of hide, legal tender nowhere.

I'd kneel at any curtain and spill it, the whole lot.
Even today, when I play back our splitting-up
I can feel how I squared my shoulders,

suddenly rich with hunger, ate two sandwiches
and wept for two years. It makes my mouth
water to think of it, every blessed time.

Lynn Davidson

Learning to Sound

The crystal-chandelier-tinkle of our old dinghy
moving across water. Our starry life

tightened across night until the bow deepened
and the hair was taut.

My mother showed me how to rosin the strings
to avoid slick spots

or silence where sound should be. I
played in a jersey brilliant with salt. I played at sea.

I carried my violin carefully up the beach
while behind me my parents

hauled the clinker into gravity
grinding it through pebbles.

On solid amber afternoons inside the pine scent
of trees I barely knew, I pitched and drew.

Claire Williamson

The Walk

1384. It is a hundred years since our children left.
~ Hamelin Town Records

Without a goodbye, my children were led away
through a crack in the Prachov Rocks,
too narrow for adults and were gone

                                        while I

scrambled a scree, crossed a bridge
to the next valley, to find them safe,
comparing boulders on the trail,
unaware of my frost-splitting panic.

I've been thinking of Hamelin.

Not the piper dressed in jester-scarlet,
hunter-green, whistling rat songs along
the River Weser. Not him.

But rather the mothers who gaze
through streaked kitchen windows
at sandstone stacks.

And I think of that old painting
showing a teardrop walled town, on a rainy day,
dwarfed by a high hill cleft open
by a muddy, rock-filled landslide,
ready to crush the town's youngsters
while the settlement's red roofs
stand stiff as open prayer books.

In the same picture, fathers punt, fish,
oblivious to the imminent disaster.

I think of that ripping yarn –
a limping lone survivor-witness,
vermin and betrayal –
told and retold
which won't be written down
for a hundred years,
explaining how it can possibly be,
that as quick as the flick of a rodent's tail,
we can lose our children.

Clare Shaw

My Mother was a Verified Miracle

My mother was church door where millions entered.
My mother was tower where four kestrels roosted –
my mother was hooded, she plunged and she hovered.
She flew at the speed of the wind, oh
my mother had wings and her voice was an organ,
she was seraph and cherub and throne and dominion.
My mother was bright with flame.

My mother was saint and my mother was martyr
and she was the light floating over the water.
My mother was whale and I rode safe inside her –
I was blessed and I came out clean
for my mother was sermon and she was the mountain
and she was the tree and the nails and the Roman
and her rafters were oak and her stone was all golden.

My mother said Let there be light
and she was the light. My mother was fruit
and we peopled the earth in her name
for my mother was sun and my mother was thunder.
My mother would get at the truth if it killed her –
she laid waste to the nations for me did my mother
and I could not run from her love

for my mother was choir, she was every bird singing
and she was the song and will not be forgotten.
My mother was angel, my mother was fallen.
She suffered the children and fed them on nothing.
My mother was bread
and my mother was broken
and she was the ark. She was darkness. The ocean.

Arundhathi Subramaniam

Song for Catabolic Women

We're bound for the ocean
and a largesse of sky
We're not looking for the truth
or living a lie

We're coming apart
we're going downhill
the fury's almost done
we've had our fill

(We're passionate, ironic
angelic, demonic
clairvoyant, rational
wildly Indian, anti-national)

We're not trying to make our peace
not itching for a fight
We don't need your shade
and we don't need your light

(We know charisma isn't contagious
and most rules are egregious)

We're catabolic women

We've known the refuge of human arms
the comfort of bathroom floors
We've stormed out of rooms
thrown open the doors

We've figured the tricks to turn rage
into celebration
We know why the oldest god dances
at every cremation

We've kissed in the rose garden
been the belles of the ball
hidden under bedcovers
and we've stood tall

We're not interested in camouflage
or self-revelation
not looking for a bargain
or an invitation

We're capable of stillness
even as we gallivant
capable of wisdom
even as we rant

Look into our eyes
you'll see we're almost through
(we can be kind but we're not really
thinking of you)

We don't remember names
and we don't do Sudoku
(we're losing EQ and IQ
forgetting to say please and thank you)

We're catabolic women

We've never ticked the right boxes
never filled out the form
our dharma is tepid
our politics lukewarm

We've had enough of earnestness
and indignation
but still keep the faith
in conversation

We're wily Easterners enough
to argue nirvana and bhakti
talk yin and yang
Shiva and Shakti

And when we don't get a visa
we fall back on astral travel
and when samsara gets intense
we simply unravel

We're unbuilding now
unperpetuating
unfortifying
disintegrating

We're caterwauling
    catastrophic
    shambolic
    cataclysmic
    catabolic women

And of course I am afraid, because the transformation of silence into language and action is an act of self-revelation, and that always seems fraught with danger. But my daughter [...] said, "Tell them about how you're never really a whole person if you remain silent, because there's always that one little piece inside you that wants to be spoken out, and if you keep ignoring it, it gets madder and madder and hotter and hotter, and if you don't speak it out one day it will just up and punch you in the mouth from the inside."

© 1984, 2007 by **Audre Lorde** - from 'Transformation of Silence', *Sister Outsider* (Crossing Press, Berkeley)

Checklist for speaking of oneself

1 – If what you have to say is important, say it and don't worry what anyone else will think.

2 – If no-one else is saying what needs to be said, open your mouth and say it. Be brave.

3 – Write a list of your achievements. Put everything on the list that matters to you, no matter how big or small.

4 – Read this list out loud to yourself.

5 – Ask a friend if you can read the list out loud to them. Better still, ask them to write a list too so that you can share your achievements and talents with each other. Dare to show each other how amazing you are.

6 – Every time something good happens, celebrate. Phone a friend and share the good news. Look at yourself in the mirror and say Well Done!

7 – Form support groups where you practise speaking of yourself. Take 5 minutes each to begin with. Use a timer so that you have the whole 5 minutes to yourself without interruption. Practise using your voice and getting used to the sound of it.

8 – Remember that sometimes the achievement you're making is just speaking your truth out loud.

9 – Put your list of achievements somewhere you can see it – and then, when you're feeling brave, put the list where others can see it too.

10 – Ask a friend what they're most proud of achieving. Ask them to tell you in detail.

11 – If you're a teacher, show this book to everyone in your class. Let them know it's okay to achieve in this world and to speak of those achievements. Show it to boys and girls, pupils who might be transitioning or choose to identify as gender neutral. It's important for everyone to be able to be proud of who they are.

Contributor Biographies

Khairani Barokka is a writer and artist. She's presented work extensively in ten countries, and is most recently co-editor of *Stairs and Whispers: D/deaf and Disabled Poets Write Back* (Nine Arches), author-illustrator of *Indigenous Species* (Tilted Axis), and author of *Rope* (Nine Arches). http://www.khairanibarokka.com/

Nazand Begikhani is Senior Research Fellow at University of Bristol, and an internationally known Kurdish poet with eight collections. She was awarded the Emma Humphreys Memorial Prize and Kurdistan Gender Equality Prize for writing and activism against gender-based violence. Selected by Forward Poetry as 'one of the best' poets of 2006 she was awarded the French Feminine Poetry prize 2012 with Simon Landrey.

Rachel Bentham has two poetry collections – *Let All Tongues Flower* and *Trust* - published by Firewater Press. She won the US International Open Poetry Contest, and has had numerous plays, docudramas and stories broadcast on BBC radio. She lectures at Bath Spa, Oxford and Bristol universities.

Judy Brown's *Crowd Sensations* (Seren, 2016) is a PBS Recommendation and was shortlisted for the Ledbury Forte prize. *Loudness* (Seren, 2011) was shortlisted for the Forward and Aldeburgh prizes for best first collection. She was poet-in-residence at the Wordsworth Trust in 2013. www.judy-brown.co.uk

Anne Caldwell is a poet and lecturer for the Open University, based in West Yorkshire. Her latest collection is *Painting the Spiral Staircase,* Cinnamon, 2016. She was shortlisted for the Rialto Poetry Pamphlet competition in 2017 and is working on a new book of prose poems.

Caroline Carver lives in Cornwall, UK. She's a National Prize winner and author of more than half a dozen books, written in various voices and accents, both men's and women's. It's fun to be a ventriloquist, but at crunch time you must stand up for who you are.

Lynn Davidson is a New Zealand writer living in Edinburgh. She writes poetry, essays and fiction. In 2016 Lynn was the recipient of a Bothy Project Residency, in 2013 she had a writing fellowship at Hawthornden Castle in Midlothian, Scotland, and in 2011 was Visiting Artist at Massey University in New Zealand.

Lucy English is a spoken word poet and novelist. She has three novels published by Fourth Estate and her collection of poetry, *Prayer to Imperfection* was published by Burning Eye in 2014. She is a Reader in Creative Writing at Bath Spa University.

Sally Evans's most recent book is *A Burrell Tapestry and a Marion Burrell Sampler*, a study of the collector William Burrell and his lifelong feud with his daughter Marion Burrell. Sally's recent ebooks *Tormaukin* and *Drip Road* about the Scottish countryside were published by Firewater Press. She is currently studying for a PhD in Creative Writing at Lancaster University.

Victoria Field is a writer and poetry therapist based in Canterbury, Kent. Her recent books include a memoir (*Baggage: A Book of Leavings*, Francis Boutle, 2016) and *The Lost Boys* (Waterloo, 2014) which won the Holyer an Gof Prize for Poetry and Drama.

Gill Hague has been an activist on violence against women for 40 years. She is Emeritus Professor of Violence against Women Studies, and a founder of the Bristol Centre for Gender and Violence Studies. She has authored/edited three poetry collections and 125 publications on gender-based violence. Gill has a Life-time Achievement Award for work on gender violence.

Alyson Hallett's latest pamphlet, *Toots* (Mariscat Press, 2017), was shortlisted for the Michael Marks Award and chosen by Jackie Kay as a summer read in *The Observer*. Collections include *Suddenly Everything* (Poetry Salzburg) and *The Stone Library* (Peterloo Poets). She lives in Bath and goes to Scotland and Albania whenever she can.

Fiona Hamilton's writing includes 'Clay Bricks' for BBC Radio 3 (2018), and poetry collections *Fractures* (Gomer Press, 2016) and *Bite Sized* (Jessica Kingsley Publishers, 2014). The latter was shortlisted for the Rubery Book Prize and performed with dancers at Bristol's Tobacco Factory Theatre. Fiona teaches at Metanoia Institute and University of Bristol.

Deborah Harvey finds inspiration for her writing in the landscapes and stories of her native West Country. Her poetry collections, *Communion* (2011), *Map Reading for Beginners* (2014), and *Breadcrumbs* (2016), are published by Indigo Dreams, while her historical novel, *Dart*, appeared under their Tamar Books imprint in 2013.

Jean Wallace Hathaway was born in a snowstorm in rural Scotland 1947, Jean loves writing and performing her poems. Broadcast, and published in BBC *Longman The Poetry of War*, collections, anthologies and independent presses including Envoi, Aireings, Weyfarers, Staple, Orbis, Smoke, Ore. Greenham-woman, installation-artist, wild-swimmer. Activist : ecology, homelessness, the arts, literacy, disarmament, equality.

Tania Hershman's debut poetry collection, *Terms & Conditions*, is published by Nine Arches Press (2017) and her third short story collection, *Some Of Us Glow More Than Others*, by Unthank Books (2017). Tania is co-author of *Writing Short Stories: A Writers' & Artists' Companion* (Bloomsbury, 2014) and curator of ShortStops (www.shortstops.info), celebrating short story activity across the UK & Ireland.

Alwyn Marriage's ten books include poetry, non-fiction and a novel. She's widely represented in magazines, anthologies and online, and gives readings all over the world. Formerly a university philosophy lecturer, Director of two international NGOs and Rockefeller Scholar, she's currently Managing Editor of Oversteps Books and research fellow at Surrey University. www.marriages.me.uk/alwyn.

Katrina Naomi has recently returned from writing in Japan on an Arts Council-sponsored project to take up a poetry residency at the Leach Pottery in St Ives. Her latest collection is *The Way the Crocodile Taught Me* (Seren, 2016). Katrina teaches for Arvon, the Poetry School and the Poetry Society. www.katrinanaomi.co.uk

Janet Paisley is an award-winning poet, author, playwright and script-writer with an international reputation. She is the recipient of a Creative Scotland award, Bafta and Royal Television Society nominations, the Peggy Ramsay award for *Refuge*, Canongate and BBC prose prizes. Her work is published in several languages, and in numerous countries.

Daisy Proctor was winner of the children's National Poetry Day competition in 2016, on the theme of 'Messages to the Planet'. She's won a Chepstow Library Prize for an essay on Michael Morpurgo. Daisy is passionate about animals and the environment. She's considering a career as a marine biologist. Daisy was born in 2009.

Dikra Ridha is a literary translator and interpreter. Her pamphlet: *'There are no Americans in Baghdad's Bird Market'* was published in 2009. She is a British-Iraqi poet based in Bath and is working on a new collection of poems and a memoir exploring her early life in North Africa.

Julie-ann Rowell's pamphlet collection *Convergence* (Brodie Press) won a PBS Award. Her collection *Letters North* was nominated for the Michael Murphy Poetry Prize for Best First Collection in Britain and Ireland in 2011. Her latest collection, *Voices in the Garden*, about Joan of Arc, is published by Lapwing Publications, Belfast.

Jo Shapcott was born in London. Poems from her three award-winning collections, *Electroplating the Baby* (1988), *Phrase Book* (1992) and *My Life Asleep* (1998) are gathered in a selected poems, *Her Book* (2000). She has won the Forward Prize for Best Collection and the National Poetry Competition (twice). In 2011 she was awarded the Queen's Gold Medal for Poetry.

Clare Shaw has two collections from Bloodaxe: *Straight Ahead* (2006) and *Head On* (2012). Her third collection, *Flood*, is published by Bloodaxe in June 2018. Often addressing political and personal conflict, her poetry is fuelled by a strong conviction in the transformative and redemptive power of language.

Penelope Shuttle's most recent collection is *Will You Walk A Little Faster?* Bloodaxe Books, 2017. She is currently working on a book-length sequence titled *Lyonesse*. In Spring 2018, in collaboration with Alyson Hallett, she publishes *Lzrd*, Indigo Dreams Publications, poems inspired by The Lizard Peninsula, Cornwall.

Cara Squires is currently studying Professional and Creative Writing at UWE Bristol. She likes candles, the colour pink, and people who are kind to each other. She has been writing since such a thing was within her capability.

Arundhathi Subramaniam was described as 'one of the finest poets writing in India today' (*The Hindu*, 20010), Arundhathi Subramaniam is the award-winning author of four books of poetry, most recently *When God is a Traveller* (Bloodaxe Books, 2014), shortlisted for the TS Eliot Prize. She is also a prose writer on spirituality and culture.

Claire Williamson's poetry collection *Visiting the Minotaur* (2018) explores bereavement, motherhood and identity. She was highly commended in the Bridport Prize (2017) and runner-up in the Neil Gunn writing competition (2017). Claire's a doctoral candidate in Creative Writing at Cardiff University and Programme Leader for the MSc in Creative Writing for Therapeutic Purposes at Metanoia Institute.

Jennifer Wong is the author of *Goldfish* (Chameleon Press, 2013). Her work has appeared in magazines including *The Rialto, The North, Stand, Oxford Poetry, Magma* (forthcoming), *Voice and Verse* and others. She also reviews books for *Poetry Review, Poetry London* and other publications. She is completing a creative writing PhD at Oxford Brookes University.